BEST OF
ITALY

Consultant Editor:
Valerie Ferguson

LORENZ BOOKS

Contents

Introduction

Italy is a country of great diversity. Its long coastline encloses a landscape of fertile plains, forest-covered mountains and arid rocks. From the hot, dry south to the cool Alpine foothills, the climate and local crops vary: rice, maize and ham are northern staples, while olives, durum wheat and tomatoes thrive in the southern heat.

Each region has distinct cultural differences, especially in culinary practices. Traditional foods are still central to the cultural identity of each region. This is partly because recipes are passed from generation to generation, rarely being written down in cookbooks, but nonetheless surviving in families for years with little or no changes made to them.

A great deal of Italian food comes from this *contadino*, or peasant, heritage. The best combines fresh ingredients with simple cooking techniques. Meats, fish and vegetables are flavoured with herbs and olive oil and often grilled or baked. Aromatic sauces can usually be assembled in the time it takes pasta to boil.

The Italian diet – high in vegetables and carbohydrates and low in animal fats – is a healthy one. It certainly tastes exceptionally good, as you will discover from the delicious recipes that follow in this book.

Ingredients

The following store cupboard ingredients are all commonly used to give Italian dishes their characteristic flavours.

PASTA

While fresh pasta is generally preferred, both for flavour and for speed of cooking, the dried product is a very valuable storecupboard ingredient. Look for the words "durum wheat" on the packet, as this is top quality pasta which produces good results.

RICE

Another popular ingredient in northern Italy is rice, which is used to make risotto. Of the special varieties grown in the area for this purpose, the best known and most widely available are arborio, vialone nano and carnaroli.

POLENTA

Coarsely ground yellow maize is a staple of the northern Italian diet.

PULSES

A typical Italian store cupboard will always contain a supply of dried, natural ingredients. There is a wide variety of dried beans and lentils, which should be stored in air-tight containers for use in soups and stews.

Below, clockwise from top: green lentils, chick-peas, porcini mushrooms, dried borlotti beans, dried cannellini beans, capers and arborio rice.

TOMATO PUREE (PASTE)

An essential if you are making a sauce from insipid fresh tomatoes! It will intensify any tomato-based sauce and will help thicken meat sauces. It will also make tomato pasta if added to the basic ingredients.

TOMATOES: CANNED PLUM OR CHOPPED

No store cupboard should be without these – invaluable for making any tomato sauce or stew when good fresh tomatoes are not available.

TOMATOES: SUN-DRIED IN OIL

These tomatoes are drained and chopped or sliced and added to tomato-based dishes to give a deeper, almost roasted tomato flavour.

OLIVE OIL

Perhaps the single most important ingredient in a modern Italian kitchen is olive oil. Buy the best cold pressed, extra virgin olive oil you can afford.

Above, clockwise from the top: green olives, bay leaves, salt cod, extra virgin olive oil, balsamic vinegar, sun-dried tomatoes and black and white peppercorns.

OLIVES

These are one of Italy's most wonderful native ingredients for antipasti or sauces and are available either black or green preserved in olive oil or brine.

BALSAMIC VINEGAR

This has only recently become widely available outside Italy. Aged slowly in wooden barrels, the finest varieties are deliciously mellow and fragrant. The taste is quite sweet and concentrated, so only a very little is needed.

PORCINI MUSHROOMS

These mushrooms are found in the woods in various parts of Europe in autumn. They can be eaten fresh, cooked or sliced thinly and dried in the sun or in special ovens.

7

Techniques

BASIC PASTA DOUGH
Impasto

INGREDIENTS
200 g/7 oz/1¾ cups plain white flour
a pinch of salt
2 eggs
15 ml/1 tbsp olive oil

1 Sift the flour and salt on to a work surface and make a well in the centre. Pour the beaten eggs and oil into the well. Gradually mix the eggs into the flour with your fingers.

2 Knead the pasta until smooth, wrap and allow to rest for at least 30 minutes before rolling out. You can also use a food processor.

Add the eggs and oil to the dry ingredients, knead and rest as above.

USING A PASTA MACHINE

1 Feed the rested dough several times through the highest setting first, then reduce the settings until the required thickness is achieved.

2 A specially designed cutter will produce fettuccine or tagliatelle. A narrower cutter will produce strands of spaghetti or tagliarini.

BASIC PIZZA DOUGH *Impasto per pizza*

This simple bread base is rolled out thinly for a traditional pizza recipe.

Makes one of the following:

1 x 25–30 cm/10–12 in
    round pizza base
4 x 13 cm/5 in
    round pizza bases
1 x 30 x 18 cm/12 x 7 in
    oblong

INGREDIENTS

175 g/6 oz/1½ cups strong white flour
1.25 ml/¼ tsp salt
5 ml/1 tsp easy-blend dried yeast
120–150 ml/4–5 fl oz/½–⅔ cup
    lukewarm water
15 ml/1 tbsp olive oil

1 Sift the flour and salt into a large mixing bowl. Stir in the yeast.

2 Make a well in the centre of the dry ingredients. Pour in the water and oil and mix with a spoon to form a soft dough.

3 Knead the dough on a lightly floured surface for about 10 minutes, until smooth and elastic.

4 Place the dough in a greased bowl and cover with clear film. Leave in a warm place to rise for about 1 hour, or until the dough has doubled in size.

5 Knock back the dough. Turn on to a lightly floured surface and knead again for 2–3 minutes. Roll out as required and place on a greased baking sheet. Push up the edge to make a rim. The dough is now ready for topping.

Minestrone

Minestrone con Pasta

A classic, substantial winter soup originally from Milan, but found in various versions around the Mediterranean coasts of Italy.

Serves 6–8

INGREDIENTS
225 g/8 oz/2 cups dried haricot beans
30 ml/2 tbsp olive oil
50 g/2 oz smoked pancetta or
    streaky bacon, diced
2 large onions, sliced
2 garlic cloves, crushed
2 medium carrots, diced
3 celery sticks, sliced
400 g/14 oz canned chopped tomatoes
2.25 litres/4 pints/10 cups beef stock
350 g/12 oz potatoes, diced
175 g/6 oz/1½ cups small pasta shapes
    (macaroni, stars, shells, etc)
225 g/8 oz green cabbage,
    thinly sliced
175 g/6 oz fine green beans, sliced
115 g/4 oz/1 cup frozen peas
45 ml/3 tbsp chopped fresh parsley
salt and freshly ground black pepper
freshly grated Parmesan cheese,
    to serve

1 Cover the beans with cold water and leave to soak overnight.

2 Heat the oil in a large saucepan and add the pancetta or bacon, onions and garlic. Cover and cook gently, stirring occasionally, for 5 minutes, until soft.

3 Add the carrots and celery and cook for 2–3 minutes, until softening but not brown.

4 Drain the haricot beans and add to the pan with the tomatoes and stock. Cover and simmer for 2–2½ hours, until the beans are tender.

5 Add the potatoes 30 minutes before the soup is finished.

6 Add the pasta shapes, sliced cabbage, green beans, peas and chopped parsley to the soup 15 minutes before it is ready. Season the soup to taste. By this time the soup should have reached a fairly thick consistency. Hand around generous amounts of grated Parmesan cheese when serving.

Wild Mushroom Soup

Zuppa di Porcini e Funghi Selvatici

Wild mushrooms are expensive. Dried porcini have an intense flavour, so use only a small quantity. The beef stock may seem unusual in a vegetable soup, but it helps to strengthen the earthy flavour of the mushrooms.

Serves 4

INGREDIENTS
25 g/1 oz/2 cups dried
    porcini (ceps) mushrooms
30 ml/2 tbsp olive oil
15 g/½ oz/1 tbsp butter
2 leeks, thinly sliced
2 shallots, roughly chopped
1 garlic clove, roughly chopped
225 g/8 oz/3 cups fresh
    wild mushrooms
about 1.2 litres/2 pints/5 cups beef stock
2.5 ml/½ tsp dried thyme
150 ml/¼ pint/⅔ cup double cream
salt and freshly ground black pepper
fresh thyme sprigs, to garnish

1 Soak the dried porcini in 250 ml/
8 fl oz/1 cup warm water for
20–30 minutes. Lift out of the liquid
and squeeze over the bowl to remove
as much of the soaking liquid as
possible. Strain and reserve the liquid.
Finely chop the porcini.

2 Heat the oil and butter in a large
saucepan until foaming. Add the
leeks, shallots and garlic and cook
gently, stirring frequently, for about
5 minutes, until they are softened
but not coloured.

3 Chop or slice the fresh mushrooms
and add to the pan. Stir over a
medium heat until they begin to
soften. Pour in the stock and bring to
the boil. Add the porcini, liquid, dried
thyme and salt and pepper. Lower the
heat, half cover and simmer gently for
30 minutes, stirring occasionally.

4 Process three-quarters of the soup
in a blender until smooth. In the
pan, add the cream and heat through.
Check seasoning and consistency, and
serve hot, garnished with thyme sprigs.

COOK'S TIP: Italian cooks would
use fresh porcini in this recipe, but
other wild mushrooms, such as
chanterelles, may be used instead.

Roasted Pepper Antipasto

Antipasto di Peperoni Arrosto

Jars of Italian mixed peppers in olive oil are now a common sight in many supermarkets. None, however, can compete with this colourful, freshly made version, perfect as a starter on its own, or with some Italian salamis and cold meats.

Serves 6

INGREDIENTS
3 red peppers
2 yellow or orange peppers
2 green peppers
50 g/2 oz/1 cup sun-dried tomatoes
    in oil, drained
1 garlic clove
30 ml/2 tbsp balsamic vinegar
75 ml/5 tbsp olive oil
few drops of chilli sauce
4 canned artichoke hearts,
    drained and sliced
salt and freshly ground
    black pepper
basil leaves, to garnish

1 Preheat the oven to 200°C/400°F/ Gas 6. Lightly oil a foil-lined baking sheet and place the whole peppers on the foil. Bake for about 45 minutes, until beginning to char. Cover with a tea towel and leave to cool for 5 minutes.

2 Slice the sun-dried tomatoes into thin strips. Thinly slice the garlic. Set the sun-dried tomatoes and garlic aside for the moment.

3 Beat together the vinegar, oil and chilli sauce, then season with a little salt and freshly ground black pepper.

4 Peel and slice the peppers. Mix with the artichokes, tomatoes and garlic. Pour over the dressing and scatter with the basil leaves.

14

Crostini

These Italian canapés consist of toasted slices of bread, spread with various toppings, such as the chicken liver pâté and prawn butter shown here.

Serves 6

INGREDIENTS
FOR THE CHICKEN LIVER PÂTÉ
150 g/5 oz/⅔ cup butter
1 small onion, finely chopped
1 garlic clove, crushed
225 g/8 oz chicken livers
4 sage leaves, chopped
salt and freshly ground black pepper

FOR THE PRAWN BUTTER
225 g/8 oz cooked, peeled prawns
2 canned anchovies, drained
115 g/4 oz/½ cup butter, softened
15 ml/1 tbsp lemon juice
15 ml/1 tbsp chopped fresh parsley
salt and freshly ground black pepper

FOR THE CROSTINI
12 slices crusty Italian bread, cut 1 cm/
    ½ in thick
75 g/3 oz/6 tbsp butter, melted

FOR THE GARNISH
sage leaves
flat leaf parsley

1 To make the chicken liver pâté, melt half the butter in a frying pan and sauté the onion and garlic until soft. Add the livers and sage and sauté for about 5 minutes, until brown and firm. Season, and blend or process with the remaining butter.

2 To make the prawn butter, chop the prawns and anchovies finely. Place in a bowl with the butter and beat together until well blended. Add the lemon juice and parsley and season with salt and pepper.

3 Preheat the oven to 200°C/400°F/ Gas 6. Place the crusty bread slices on one or two baking sheets and brush them with the melted butter.

4 Bake for 8–10 minutes, until pale golden. Spread half the hot crostini with the chicken liver pâté and the rest with the prawn butter, garnishing with sage and parsley, respectively. Serve the crostini at once.

COOK'S TIP: Both the chicken liver pâté and the prawn butter can be made ahead of serving, but should be used within two days. Cover both toppings closely and store them in the fridge.

Spaghetti with Bolognese Meat Sauce *Spaghetti Bolognese*

This great meat sauce is a speciality of Bologna. It is delicious with tagliatelle or short pasta, such as penne or conchiglie, as well as spaghetti, and is indispensable in baked lasagne. It keeps well in the fridge for several days and can also be frozen.

Serves 6

INGREDIENTS
25 g/1 oz/2 tbsp butter
60 ml/4 tbsp olive oil
1 medium onion, finely chopped
25 g/1 oz/2 tbsp pancetta or unsmoked
   bacon, finely chopped
1 carrot, finely sliced
1 stick celery, finely sliced
1 clove garlic, finely chopped
350 g/12 oz lean minced beef
150 ml/¼ pint/⅔ cup red wine
120 ml/4 fl oz/½ cup milk
1 x 400 g/14 oz can plum tomatoes,
   chopped, with their juice
1 bay leaf
¼ tsp fresh thyme leaves
salt and freshly ground
   black pepper
450 g/1 lb dried spaghetti

1 Heat the butter and oil in a heavy-based saucepan. Add the onion and cook over moderate heat for 3–4 minutes. Add the pancetta or bacon, and cook until the onion is translucent. Stir in the carrot, celery and garlic. Continue to cook for 3–4 minutes more.

2 Add the beef and stir with a fork until the meat loses its red colour. Season with salt and pepper.

3 Pour in the wine, increase the heat slightly and cook for 4 minutes. Add the milk and cook until it has evaporated.

4 Stir in the tomatoes with their juice, and the herbs. Bring the sauce to the boil. Reduce the heat to low, and simmer uncovered for 1½–2 hours, stirring occasionally. Adjust the seasoning before serving.

5 Meanwhile, cook the spaghetti in a large pan of rapidly boiling, salted water for 10–12 minutes, or until it is al dente. Drain and serve with the sauce.

Spaghetti with Clams

Spaghetti alle Vongole

This quick and tasty pasta dish is full of the flavour of the sea.

Serves 4

INGREDIENTS
30 ml/2 tbsp olive oil
1 onion, very finely chopped
2 garlic cloves, crushed
400 g/14 oz can chopped tomatoes
150 ml/¼ pint/⅔ cup dry white wine
150 g/5 oz jar or can clams in natural juice,
    drained with juice reserved
350 g/12 oz dried spaghetti
30 ml/2 tbsp finely chopped fresh flat leaf
    parsley, plus extra to garnish
salt and freshly ground black pepper

1 Heat the olive oil in a large, heavy saucepan. Add the finely chopped onion and cook gently, stirring frequently for about 5 minutes, until softened, but not brown.

2 Stir in the garlic, chopped tomatoes, white wine and reserved clam juice, with salt to taste. Season generously with black pepper.

3 Bring to the boil, stirring continuously, then lower the heat. Cover the pan and simmer the sauce gently for about 20 minutes, stirring from time to time.

4 Meanwhile, coil the spaghetti into a large saucepan of rapidly boiling salted water and cook for 10–12 minutes or until it is al dente.

5 Drain the spaghetti thoroughly. Add the clams and finely chopped parsley to the tomato sauce and heat through, then taste for seasoning. Tip the drained spaghetti into a warmed serving bowl, pour over the tomato sauce and toss to mix. Serve at once, sprinkled with more parsley.

VARIATION: You could use 350 g/12 oz fresh clams. Cook in the olive oil until opened. Remove with a slotted spoon and discard any which have not opened.

COOK'S TIP: The tomato sauce can be made several days ahead of time and kept in the fridge. Add the clams and heat them through at the last minute – but don't let them boil or they will toughen.

Pasta with Cream & Parmesan

Pasta Alfredo

This popular, classic pasta dish originated in Rome.

Serves 3–4

INGREDIENTS

350 g/12 oz dried fettuccine
25 g/1 oz/2 tbsp butter
300 ml/½ pint/1¼ cups double cream
50g/2 oz/⅔ cup grated Parmesan cheese, plus
  extra to serve
30 ml/2 tbsp finely chopped fresh flat leaf
  parsley, plus extra to garnish
salt and freshly ground black pepper

1 Cook the fettuccine in rapidly
  salted water until al dente.

2 Melt the butter in a large
  flameproof casserole and add the
cream and Parmesan, with salt and
pepper. Stir over a medium heat until
the cheese has melted and the sauce
has thickened.

3 Drain the fettuccine and add it to
  the sauce with the parsley. Fold the
pasta and sauce together over a
medium heat. Grind more pepper over
and garnish with the extra parsley.
Serve at once, with a bowl of grated
Parmesan handed round separately.

Pasta with Pesto Sauce

Salsa al Pesto (alla Genovese)

There is nothing more evocative of the warmth of Italy than a good home-made pesto. Serve generous spoonfuls with your favourite pasta.

Serves 3–4

INGREDIENTS
50 g/2 oz/2 cups tightly packed
  basil leaves
2 garlic cloves, crushed
30 ml/2 tbsp pine nuts
120 ml/4 fl oz/½ cup olive oil
40g/1½ oz/½ cup finely grated
  Parmesan cheese
salt and freshly ground
  black pepper

1 Using a pestle and mortar, grind the basil, garlic, pine nuts and seasoning to a fine paste.

2 Transfer the mixture to a bowl and whisk in the oil a little at a time.

3 Add the cheese and blend well. Adjust the seasoning to taste.

4 Alternatively, place the basil, garlic, pine nuts, salt and freshly ground black pepper in a food processor and grind the ingredients together until the mixture is as fine as possible.

5 Then, with the food processor motor running, add the olive oil in a thin stream until the mixture has formed a smooth paste.

6 Add the Parmesan cheese and pulse quickly 3–4 times. Season if necessary and heat the pesto through gently. Add to pasta and serve.

VARIATION: Pesto also makes an excellent dressing on small new potatoes. Serve while still hot or allow to cool to room temperature.

Three-cheese Lasagne

Lasagne ai Tre Formaggi

The Ricotta, Mozzarella and Parmesan cheeses make this lasagne quite expensive, so reserve it for a special occasion.

Serves 6–8

INGREDIENTS

30 ml/2 tbsp olive oil
1 onion, finely chopped
1 carrot, finely chopped
1 celery stick, finely chopped
1 garlic clove, crushed
675 g/1½ lb minced beef
400 g/14 oz can chopped tomatoes
300 ml/½ pint/1¼ cups beef stock
300 ml/½ pint/1¼ cups red wine
30 ml/2 tbsp sun-dried tomato paste
10 ml/2 tsp dried oregano
9 sheets no-precook lasagne
450 g/1 lb/2 cups Mozzarella cheese, sliced
450 g/1 lb/2 cups Ricotta cheese
115 g/4 oz/1¼ - 1½ cups freshly grated
    Parmesan cheese
salt and freshly ground black pepper

1 Heat the oil and sauté the onion, carrot, celery and garlic, stirring frequently for 10 minutes, until softened. Add the beef and cook until it changes colour, stirring constantly and breaking up the meat.

2 Add the tomatoes, stock, wine, tomato paste, oregano and salt and pepper and bring to the boil, stirring. Cover, lower the heat and simmer gently, stirring occasionally, for 1 hour.

3 Preheat the oven to 190°C/375°F/ Gas 5. Adjust the seasoning, then ladle one-third of the meat sauce into a 23 x 33-cm/9 x 13 in ovenproof dish and cover with 3 sheets of lasagne. Arrange one third of the Mozzarella slices over the top, dot with one-third of the Ricotta, then sprinkle with one third of the Parmesan.

4 Repeat these layers twice more, then bake for 40 minutes until the top is golden brown and bubbling. Leave to cool for 10 minutes before serving with a crisp salad.

COOK'S TIP: If you are serving this dish to children you could omit the red wine and double the quantity of beef stock.

Four Seasons Pizza

Pizza Quattro Stagioni

This pizza is divided into quarters, each with a different topping.

Serves 2–4

INGREDIENTS

FOR THE TOMATO SAUCE
15 ml/1 tbsp olive oil
1 onion, finely chopped
1 garlic clove, crushed
400 g/14 oz can chopped tomatoes
15 ml/1 tbsp tomato purée
15 ml/1 tbsp chopped fresh herbs, such as
    parsley, thyme, basil and oregano
pinch of sugar
salt and freshly ground black pepper

FOR THE TOPPING
45 ml/3 tbsp olive oil
50 g/2 oz button mushrooms, sliced
1 25–30 cm/10–12 inch round pizza base
50 g/2 oz Parma ham
6 pitted black olives, chopped
4 bottled artichoke hearts in oil, drained
3 canned anchovy fillets, drained
50 g/2 oz/¼ cup Mozzarella, thinly sliced
8 fresh basil leaves, shredded
freshly ground black pepper

1 Heat the oil and sauté the onion and garlic for 5 minutes, until softened. Add the tomatoes, tomato purée, herbs, sugar and seasoning. Simmer, uncovered, stirring occasionally, for 15–20 minutes, or until the tomatoes have reduced to a thick pulp. Set aside to cool.

2 Preheat the oven to 220°C/425°F/ Gas 7. Heat 15 ml/1 tbsp of the oil in a frying pan and fry the mushrooms until all the juices have evaporated. Leave to cool.

3 Brush the pizza base with half the remaining oil. Spread over the tomato sauce and mark into four equal sections with a knife. Arrange the mushrooms over one section.

4 Cut the Parma ham into strips and arrange with the olives on another section of the pizza base.

5 Thinly slice the artichoke hearts and arrange over a third section. Halve the anchovies lengthways and arrange with the Mozzarella over the fourth section.

6 Scatter over the basil. Drizzle over the remaining oil and season with black pepper. Bake for 15–20 minutes until crisp and golden.

Tomato & Anchovy Pizza

Pizza alla Napoletana

This pizza is a speciality of Naples and is simple to prepare.

Serves 2–3

INGREDIENTS
25–30 cm/10–12 inch round
  pizza base
30 ml/2 tbsp olive oil
6 plum tomatoes
2 garlic cloves, chopped
115 g/4 oz/1 cup grated
  Mozzarella cheese
50 g/2 oz can anchovy fillets,
  drained and chopped
15 ml/1 tbsp chopped fresh
  oregano
30 ml/2 tbsp freshly grated
  Parmesan cheese
freshly ground black pepper

2 Peel, seed and roughly chop the tomatoes. Spoon the tomatoes over the pizza base and sprinkle the chopped garlic over the top.

3 Mix the Mozzarella with the anchovies and scatter over.

1 Preheat the oven to 220°C/425°F/ Gas 7. Brush the pizza base with 15 ml/1 tbsp of the oil. Put the tomatoes in a bowl and pour over boiling water. Leave for 30 seconds, then plunge into cold water.

4 Sprinkle over the oregano and Parmesan. Drizzle over the remaining oil and season with black pepper. Bake for 15–20 minutes, until crisp and golden. Serve immediately.

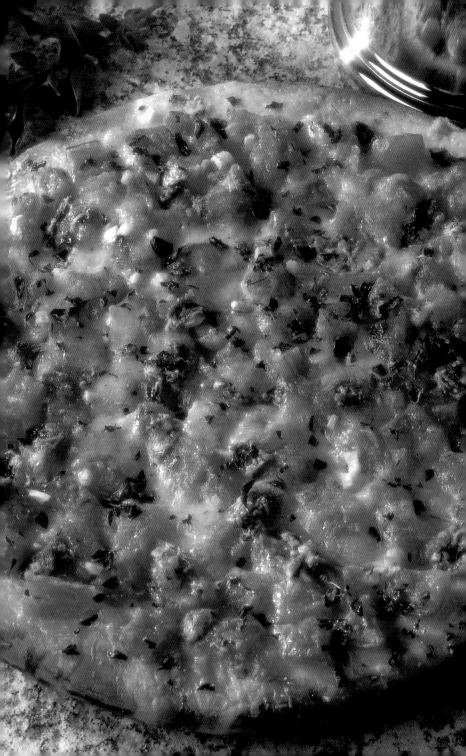

Fresh Tuna & Tomato Stew

Stufato di Tonno e Pomodori

Serve this deliciously simple dish Italian-style, with polenta or pasta.

Serves 4

INGREDIENTS
12 baby onions, peeled
900 g/2 lb ripe tomatoes
675 g/1½ lb fresh tuna
45 ml/3 tbsp olive oil
2 garlic cloves, crushed
45 ml/3 tbsp chopped fresh herbs
2 bay leaves
2.5 ml/½ tsp caster sugar
30 ml/2 tbsp sun-dried tomato paste
150 ml/¼ pint/⅔ cup dry white wine
salt and freshly ground black pepper
baby courgettes and fresh herbs, to garnish

1 Leave the onions whole and cook in a pan of boiling water for 4–5 minutes, until softened. Drain. Plunge the tomatoes into boiling water for 30 seconds, then refresh in cold water. Peel the flesh and roughly chop.

2 Cut the tuna into 2.5 cm/1 in chunks. Heat the oil in a frying pan and fry the tuna until brown. Drain.

3 Add the onions, garlic, tomatoes, chopped herbs, bay leaves, sugar, tomato paste and wine and bring to the boil, breaking up the tomatoes with a wooden spoon.

4 Reduce the heat and simmer gently for 5 minutes. Return the drained fish to the pan and cook for a further 5 minutes. Season and serve hot, garnished with baby courgettes and fresh herbs.

VARIATION: Two mackerel make a good alternative to the tuna. Fillet them and cut into chunks or simply lay the whole fish over the sauce and cook, covered with a lid. Sage, rosemary and oregano all go extremely well with this dish. Choose one or use a mixture of your two favourite herbs.

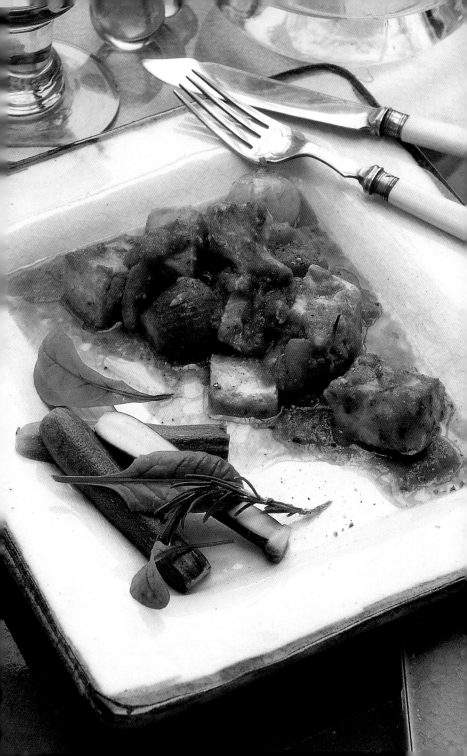

Pan-fried Red Mullet with Basil & Citrus

Triglia in Padella con Basilico e Agrume

Red mullet is popular all over the Mediterranean. This Italian recipe combines it with oranges and lemons, which grow in abundance.

Serves 4

INGREDIENTS

4 red mullet, about 225 g/8 oz each, filleted
90 ml/6 tbsp olive oil
10 peppercorns, crushed
2 oranges, one peeled and sliced
    and one squeezed, reserving the juice
1 lemon
30 ml/2 tbsp plain flour
15 g/½ oz/1 tbsp butter
2 drained canned anchovies, chopped
60 ml/4 tbsp shredded fresh basil
salt and freshly ground black pepper

1 Place the fish fillets in a shallow dish in a single layer. Pour over the olive oil and sprinkle with the crushed peppercorns. Lay the orange slices on top of the fish. Cover the dish, and leave to marinate in the fridge for at least 4 hours.

2 Halve the lemon. Remove and discard the skin and pith from one half, using a small sharp knife, and slice thinly. Squeeze the juice from the other lemon half.

3 Lift the fish out of the marinade and pat dry on kitchen paper. Reserve the marinade and orange slices. Season the fish with salt and pepper and dust lightly with flour.

4 Heat 45ml/3 tbsp of the marinade in a frying pan. Add the fish and fry for 2 minutes on each side. Remove from the pan and keep warm. Discard the marinade that is left in the pan.

5 Melt the butter in the pan with any of the remaining original marinade. Add the anchovies and cook until completely softened.

6 Stir in the orange and lemon juice, adjust the seasoning and simmer until slightly reduced. Stir in the basil. Pour the sauce over the fish and garnish with the reserved orange slices and the lemon slices.

COOK'S TIP: If red mullet is unavailable, or if you prefer, you can use fillets of other types of fish for this dish. Try it with lemon sole, haddock or hake.

Roast Chicken with Fennel

Pollo Arrosto con Finocchio

Use round rather than long fennel bulbs for this dish.

Serves 4–5

INGREDIENTS
1.5 kg/3½ lb roasting chicken
1 onion, quartered
120 ml/4 fl oz/½ cup olive oil
2 medium fennel bulbs
1 clove garlic, peeled
pinch of freshly grated nutmeg
3–4 thin slices pancetta or bacon
120 ml/4 fl oz/½ cup dry white wine
salt and freshly ground black pepper

1 Preheat the oven to 180°C/350°F/
Gas 4. Rinse the chicken in cold
water. Pat it dry inside and out with
paper towels. Sprinkle the cavity with
salt and pepper. Place the onion
quarters in the cavity. Rub the chicken
with about 45 ml/3 tbsp of the olive
oil. Place in a roasting tin.

2 Cut the green fronds from the
tops of the fennel bulbs. Finely
chop the fronds with the garlic. Place
in a small bowl and mix with the
freshly grated nutmeg. Season with
salt and pepper. Sprinkle the fennel
mixture over the chicken, pressing it
on to the oiled skin. Cover the breast
with the slices of pancetta or bacon.
Sprinkle with 30 ml/2 tbsp of olive
oil. Place in the centre of the oven
and roast for 30 minutes.

3 Meanwhile, boil or steam the
fennel bulbs until just tender.
Remove from the heat and cut into
quarters or sixths lengthways. After
the chicken has been cooking for
30 minutes, remove the tin from the
oven. Baste the roasted chicken with
any oils in the tin.

4 Arrange the fennel pieces around
the chicken. Sprinkle the fennel
with the remaining oil. Pour about
half the wine over the chicken, and
return the tin to the oven. After 30
minutes more, baste the chicken again.
Pour on the remaining wine. Cook for
15–20 minutes more. To test, prick the
thigh with a fork. If the juices run
clear, the chicken is cooked. Transfer
the chicken to a serving platter and
arrange the fennel around it.

Chicken with Ham & Cheese

Petti di pollo alla Bolognese

This tasty combination comes from Emilia-Romagna.

Serves 4

INGREDIENTS

4 small, skinless, boneless chicken breasts
flour seasoned with salt and freshly ground
   black pepper, for dredging
50 g/2 oz/4 tbsp butter
3–4 leaves fresh sage
4 thin slices prosciutto crudo,
   or cooked ham, cut in half
50 g/2 oz/⅔ cup freshly grated
   Parmesan cheese

1 Cut each breast in half lengthways to make two flat fillets. Dredge the chicken in the seasoned flour, and shake off the excess.

2 Preheat the grill. Heat the butter with the sage leaves in a large, heavy frying pan. Add the chicken breasts in one layer, and cook over low to moderate heat for about 15 minutes, turning a few times as necessary, until golden brown and cooked on both sides.

3 Remove the chicken from the heat and arrange on a flameproof serving dish or grill pan. Place one piece of ham on each chicken fillet and top with the grated Parmesan. Grill for 3–4 minutes, or until the cheese has melted and is just beginning to bubble. Serve at once.

Meatballs with Fontina

Polpettine con Fontina

Meatballs are easy to stuff with nuggets of creamy cheese that melt during cooking. In this dish, the meatballs are filled with Fontina cubes and then rolled in crumbs and fried.

Serves 6–8

INGREDIENTS

500 g/1¼ lb lean minced beef
500 g/1¼ lb lean minced pork
3 garlic cloves, crushed
grated rind and juice of 1 lemon
2 slices of day-old bread, crumbled
40 g/1½ oz/½ cup freshly grated
    Parmesan cheese
2.5 ml/½ tsp ground cinnamon
5 ml/1 tsp dried oregano
2 eggs, beaten
150 g/5 oz Fontina cheese, cut into 16 cubes
115–150 g/4–5 oz/1–1¼ cups natural-
    coloured dried breadcrumbs
olive oil, for shallow frying
5 ml/1 tsp salt
ground black pepper
fresh herbs and freshly grated
    Parmesan cheese, to garnish
cooked pasta, a mixed leaf salad and
    tomato sauce, to serve

1 Preheat the oven to 180°C/350°F/ Gas 4. Put the minced beef and pork with the garlic, lemon rind and juice, fresh breadcrumbs, Parmesan, cinnamon and oregano in a bowl. Stir in the beaten eggs and mix well. Add the salt and a generous helping of freshly ground black pepper.

2 Using clean hands occasionally dipped into cold water, knead the mixture to ensure all the ingredients are well distributed, then shape it into 16 balls. Cup each ball in turn in your hand and press a piece of Fontina into the centre. Reshape the ball, making sure the cheese is well-covered.

3 Roll the meatballs in the dried crumbs. Heat the olive oil in a large frying pan. Add the meatballs in batches and cook them quickly all over until lightly browned and sealed. Transfer them to a roasting tin and bake for 20 minutes or until cooked through. Garnish with fresh herbs and Parmesan and serve with pasta, salad and tomato sauce.

VARIATION: Use cubes of Raclette, Gouda or Monterey Jack instead of Fontina to fill the meatballs.

Roast Lamb with Rosemary
Agnello Arrosto al Rosmarino

In Italy, lamb is traditionally served at Easter. This simple roast owes its wonderful flavour to the fresh rosemary and garlic. It makes the perfect Sunday lunch at any time of year, served with fresh vegetables.

Serves 4

INGREDIENTS
½ leg of lamb, about 1.4 kg/3 lb
2 garlic cloves, cut lengthways into
　　thin slivers
105 ml/7 tbsp olive oil
leaves from 4 sprigs of fresh rosemary,
　　finely chopped
about 250 ml/8 fl oz/1 cup lamb or
　　vegetable stock
675 g/1½ lb potatoes,
　　cut into 2.5 cm/1 in cubes
a few fresh sage leaves, chopped
salt and freshly ground
　　black pepper
lightly cooked baby carrots,
　　to serve

1 Preheat the oven to 230°C/450°F/ Gas 8. Using the point of a sharp knife, make deep incisions in the leg of lamb, especially near the bone, and insert the slivers of garlic. Put the lamb in a roasting tin and rub it all over with 45 ml/3 tbsp of the olive oil. Sprinkle over about half of the chopped fresh rosemary, patting it on firmly, and season with plenty of salt and freshly ground black pepper. Roast the lamb in the oven for 30 minutes, turning it over once.

2 Lower the oven temperature to 190°C/375°F/Gas 5. Turn the lamb over again and add 120 ml/4 fl oz/ ½ cup of the stock. Roast for a further 1¼–1½ hours, until the lamb is tender, turning the joint two or three times more and adding the rest of the stock in two or three batches. Baste the lamb each time it is turned.

3 Meanwhile, put the potatoes in a separate roasting tin and toss with the remaining oil and rosemary, and the sage. Roast, on the same shelf as the lamb if possible, for 45 minutes, turning the potatoes several times until they are golden and tender.

COOK'S TIP: If you would like to make a thin gravy to serve with the roast lamb, strain the cooking juices at the end, and combine them with extra lamb or vegetable stock and some red wine.

4 Transfer the lamb to a carving board, tent with foil and leave in a warm place for 10 minutes so that the flesh firms for easier carving. Serve whole or carved into thin slices, surrounded by the potatoes and accompanied by baby carrots.

Calf's Liver with Balsamic Vinegar

Fegato di Vitello all'Aceto Balsamico

This sweet and sour liver dish is a speciality of Venice. Serve it very simply, with green beans sprinkled with browned breadcrumbs.

Serves 2

INGREDIENTS
15 ml/1 tbsp plain flour
2.5 ml/½ tsp finely chopped fresh sage
4 thin slices of calf's liver,
    cut into serving pieces
45 ml/3 tbsp olive oil
25 g/1 oz/2 tbsp butter
2 small red onions, sliced and
    separated into rings
150 ml/¼ pint/⅔ cup dry white wine
45 ml/3 tbsp balsamic vinegar
pinch of sugar
salt and freshly ground black pepper
fresh sprigs of sage, to garnish
green beans sprinkled with browned
    breadcrumbs, to serve

1 Spread out the flour in a shallow bowl. Season it with the sage and plenty of salt and pepper. Turn the liver in the flour until well coated.

2 Heat 30 ml/2 tbsp of the oil with half the butter in a wide, heavy-based saucepan or frying pan until foaming. Add the onion rings and cook gently, stirring frequently, for about 5 minutes until softened but not coloured. Remove and set aside.

3 Heat the remaining oil and butter until foaming, and cook the liver over medium heat for 2–3 minutes each side. It quickly turns tough, but should be served slightly underdone and pink, like a rare steak. Transfer to heated plates and keep hot.

4 Add the wine and vinegar to the pan, then stir to mix with the pan juices and sediment. Add the onions and sugar and heat through, stirring. Spoon over the liver, garnish with sage and serve at once with the beans.

Risotto with Asparagus

Risotto con Asparagi

This is an elegant risotto to make when asparagus is in season.

Serves 4–5

INGREDIENTS

225 g/8 oz asparagus, lower stalks peeled
750 ml/1¼ pints/3 cups vegetable stock
65 g/2½ oz/5 tbsp butter
1 small onion, finely chopped
400 g/14 oz/2 cups medium-grain
   risotto rice, such as arborio
75 g/3 oz/1 cup freshly grated
   Parmesan cheese
salt and freshly ground black pepper

1 Blanch the asparagus in a pan of boiling water for 5 minutes. Lift the asparagus out, reserving the cooking water. Rinse under cold water. Drain and cut diagonally into 4 cm/1½ in pieces. Keep the tip and next-highest sections separate from the stalk sections.

2 Place the stock in a saucepan, adding 900 ml/1½ pints/3¾ cups of the asparagus cooking water. Heat the liquid to simmering, and keep it hot until it is needed.

3 Heat two-thirds of the butter in a large heavy frying pan or casserole. Add the onion and cook until it is soft and golden. Stir in all the asparagus except the top two sections. Cook for 2–3 minutes. Add the rice, mixing well to coat it with butter for 1–2 minutes.

4 Stir in half a ladleful of the hot liquid. Using a wooden spoon, stir constantly until the liquid has been absorbed. Continue stirring and adding the vegetable stock, a little at a time, for about 10 minutes.

5 Adding the remaining asparagus sections, continue cooking, stirring and adding the liquid until the rice is tender but still firm to the bite. If you run out of stock before the rice is tender, use hot water, but do not worry if the rice is cooked before you have used up all the stock.

6 Stir in the remaining butter and the grated Parmesan off the heat. Grind in a little black pepper, and taste again for salt.

VARIATION: You could roast the asparagus spears, coated in a little olive oil and sea salt, for 8 minutes.

Spinach & Ricotta Gnocchi

Gnocchi di Ricotta e Spinaci

The success of this dish lies in not overworking the mixture, to achieve delicious, light mouthfuls.

Serves 4

INGREDIENTS
900 g/2 lb fresh spinach
350 g/12 oz/1½ cups ricotta cheese
60 ml/4 tbsp freshly grated
   Parmesan cheese, plus extra to serve
3 eggs, beaten
1.5 ml/¼ tsp grated nutmeg
45–60 ml/3–4 tbsp plain flour
115 g/4 oz/8 tbsp butter, melted
salt and freshly ground
   black pepper

1 Place the spinach in a large pan and cook for 5 minutes, until wilted. Leave to cool, then squeeze the spinach as dry as possible. Process in a blender or food processor, then transfer to a bowl.

2 Add the Ricotta, Parmesan, eggs and nutmeg. Season with salt and pepper and mix together. Add enough flour to make the mixture into a soft dough. Using your hands, shape the mixture into 7.5 cm/3 in "sausages" (gnocchi), then dust lightly with flour.

3 Bring a large pan of salted water to the boil. Gently slide the gnocchi into the water and cook for 1–2 minutes, until they float to the surface. Remove the gnocchi with a slotted spoon and transfer to a warm dish. Pour over the melted butter and sprinkle with extra Parmesan cheese. Serve at once.

Polenta Baked with Cheese

Polenta Pasticciata con Formaggio

Cold polenta can be cut into slices and baked in layers with cheese and other ingredients. The traditional way of cutting it is with a wooden knife or a piece of thick thread.

Serves 4–6

INGREDIENTS
250 g/9 oz/2 cups quick cook
    polenta flour
75 g/3 oz/6 tbsp butter
1 litre/1¾ pints/4 cups water
45 ml/3 tbsp olive oil
2 medium onions, thinly sliced
pinch of grated nutmeg
150 g/5 oz/¾ cup Mozzarella
    or mature Cheddar cheese,
    cut into thin slices
45 ml/3 tbsp finely chopped
    fresh parsley
35 g/1½ oz/⅓ cup freshly grated
    Parmesan cheese
salt and freshly ground black pepper

1 To make the polenta, bring the water to the boil in a large saucepan. Pour the polenta into the pan in a steady stream, whisking constantly. Cook, stirring occasionally, for 5–7 minutes until it pulls away from the side of the saucepan.

2 Stir a third of the butter into the polenta. Sprinkle a work surface with water. Spread the polenta in a layer 1 cm/½ in thick. Allow to cool. Cut into 6 cm/2½ in rounds.

3 Heat the oil in a medium saucepan with 15 g/½ oz/1 tbsp of the remaining butter. Add the onions, and sauté, stirring occasionally, over low heat until soft.

4 Season the onions with nutmeg, salt and pepper. Preheat the oven to 190°C/375°F/Gas 5. Butter an ovenproof dish. Spread a few of the onion slices in the bottom of the dish. Cover with a layer of the polenta rounds. Dot with butter.

5 Add a layer of the sliced Mozzarella or Cheddar, and a sprinkling of parsley and Parmesan. Season with salt and pepper. Make another layer of the onions, and continue the layers in order, ending with the Parmesan. Dot the top with butter. Bake for 20–25 minutes, or until the cheese has melted. Serve immediately.

Sweet Pepper & Courgette Frittata

Frittata con Peperoni Dolci e Zucchine

Eggs, cheese and vegetables form the basis of this excellent Italian supper dish. Served cold, in wedges, it makes tasty picnic fare, too.

Serves 4

INGREDIENTS
45ml/3 tbsp olive oil
1 red onion, thinly sliced
1 large red pepper, seeded and thinly sliced
1 large yellow pepper, seeded and
   thinly sliced
2 garlic cloves, crushed
1 medium courgette, thinly sliced
6 eggs
150 g/5 oz/1¼ cups freshly grated
   Italian cheese, such as Fontina,
   Provolone or Taleggio
salt and freshly ground black pepper
dressed mixed salad leaves, to garnish

2 Add the remaining oil to the pan. Add the garlic and courgette slices and stir constantly, for 5 minutes.

3 Beat the eggs with salt and pepper in a bowl. Mix in the cheese.

4 Pour the egg and cheese mixture over the vegetables, stirring lightly to mix. Make sure that the base of the pan is evenly covered. Cook over a low heat until just set.

5 Traditionally, a frittata is inverted on to a plate and returned to the pan upside-down to cook the top, but it may be easier to brown the top lightly under a hot grill for a few minutes (protect the pan handle, if necessary). Allow the frittata to stand in the pan for about 5 minutes before cutting. This is delicious served hot or cold, with a salad garnish.

1 Heat 30 ml/2 tbsp of the oil in a large, heavy-based frying pan. Fry the onion and pepper slices over a low heat for about 10 minutes, until they have just softened.

Baked Fennel with Parmesan Cheese

Finocchio Gratinato

Fennel is widely eaten in Italy, and combines well with the sharpness of Parmesan in this simple dish.

Serves 4–6

INGREDIENTS
1 kg/2¼ lb fennel bulbs,
  washed and cut in half
50 g/2 oz/4 tbsp butter
40 g/1½ oz/½ cup freshly grated
  Parmesan cheese

1 Cook the fennel in boiling water until just soft. Drain. Preheat the oven to 200°C/400°F/Gas 6.

2 Cut the fennel bulbs lengthways into 4 or 6 pieces. Place them in a buttered baking dish.

3 Dot with butter. Sprinkle with the grated Parmesan. Bake in the oven for 20 minutes, until the cheese is golden brown. Serve at once.

VARIATION: For a more substantial version, sprinkle 75 g/3 oz chopped mushrooms over the fennel before topping with the cheese.

Roast Mushroom Caps

Funghi Arrosto

Hunting for edible wild mushrooms is an Italian passion. Porcini, which grow in forests, are most prized.

Serves 4

INGREDIENTS
4 large mushroom caps, such as porcini
2 cloves garlic, chopped
45 ml/3 tbsp finely chopped fresh parsley
salt and freshly ground black pepper
extra virgin olive oil, for sprinkling

1 Preheat the oven to 190°C/375°F/ Gas 5. Carefully wipe the mushrooms clean with a damp cloth or paper towel. Cut off the stems. (Save them for soup if not too woody.) Oil an ovenproof dish large enough to hold the mushrooms in one layer.

2 Place the mushroom caps in the dish, smooth side down. Mix garlic and parsley and sprinkle on top.

3 Season with salt and pepper. Sprinkle the stuffing with oil. Bake for 20–25 minutes. Serve at once.

Right: Baked Fennel with Parmesan Cheese; Roast Mushroom Caps.

Stuffed Aubergines

Melanzane Ripiene alla Ligure

This typical Ligurian dish is spiked with paprika and allspice.

Serves 4

INGREDIENTS
2 aubergines, about 225 g/8 oz each
275 g/10 oz potatoes, peeled and diced
30 ml/2 tbsp olive oil
1 small onion, finely chopped
1 garlic clove, finely chopped
good pinch of ground allspice and paprika
1 egg, beaten
40 g/1½ oz/½ cup freshly grated
    Parmesan cheese
15 ml/1 tbsp fresh white breadcrumbs
salt and freshly ground black pepper
fresh mint sprigs, to garnish
salad leaves, to serve

1 Bring a large saucepan of lightly salted water to the boil. Add the aubergines, stalks removed, and cook for 5 minutes, turning frequently. Remove with a slotted spoon and set aside. Cook the potatoes in the pan for 20 minutes until soft.

2 Meanwhile, cut the aubergines in half lengthways and gently scoop out the flesh with a small, sharp knife and a spoon, leaving 5 mm/¼ in of the shell intact. Select an ovenproof dish that will hold the aubergine shells snugly in a single layer. Brush it lightly with oil. Put the shells in the dish and chop the aubergine flesh roughly.

3 Heat the oil in a frying pan, add the onion and sauté, stirring frequently, until softened. Add the chopped aubergine flesh and the garlic. Cook, stirring frequently, for 6–8 minutes. Tip into a bowl. Preheat the oven to 190°C/375°F/Gas 5.

4 Drain and mash the cooked potatoes. Add to the aubergine mixture with the spices and beaten egg. Set aside 15 ml/1 tbsp of the Parmesan cheese and add the rest to the aubergine mixture. Stir in salt and freshly ground pepper to taste.

5 Spoon the aubergine and potato mixture into the aubergine shells. Mix the breadcrumbs with the reserved Parmesan cheese and sprinkle this mixture over the stuffed aubergines. Bake in the oven for 40–45 minutes, until the topping is crisp and golden. Garnish with mint sprigs and serve with salad leaves.

Rocket, Pear & Parmesan
Salad *Insalata di Pere, Parmigiano e Rucola*

This is a simple but sophisticated salad with a hint of sweetness.

Serves 4

INGREDIENTS
3 ripe pears, Williams or Packhams
10 ml/2 tsp lemon juice
45 ml/3 tbsp hazelnut or walnut oil
115 g/4 oz rocket
75 g/3 oz/1 cup Parmesan
  cheese shavings
freshly ground black pepper
open-textured bread, to serve

1 Peel, core and thickly slice the
pears. Moisten with lemon juice to
keep the flesh white.

2 Combine the nut oil with the
sliced pears. Add the rocket leaves
and toss well to coat.

3 Turn the salad out on to 4 small
plates and top with shavings of
Parmesan cheese. Season with freshly
ground black pepper and serve with
open-textured bread.

COOK'S TIP: If you are unable to
buy rocket easily, you can grow your
own from early spring to late
summer.

Three-colour Salad

Insalata Tricolore

This salad dish depends for its success on the quality of its ingredients.

Serves 2

INGREDIENTS
150 g/5 oz/¾ cup Mozzarella di bufala
    cheese, thinly sliced
4 large plum tomatoes,
    sliced
sea salt flakes
1 large avocado
about 12 basil leaves or a small handful of
    flat leaf parsley leaves
45–60 ml/3–4 tbsp extra virgin olive oil
freshly ground black pepper
ciabatta or other Italian bread,
    to serve

1 Arrange the cheese and tomatoes on two plates. Sprinkle with sea salt to draw out some of the tomato juices. Set aside for about 30 minutes.

2 Just before serving, cut the avocado in half and twist to separate. Stone and remove the peel. Slice the avocado flesh crossways into half moons.

3 Place the avocado on the salad, then sprinkle with the basil or parsley. Drizzle over the oil, add more salt if liked and black pepper. Serve at room temperature, with Italian bread.

Italian Trifle *Zuppa Inglese*

Known in Italy as "English Soup", this is nonetheless an Italian classic.

Serves 6–8

INGREDIENTS
475 ml/16 fl oz/2 cups milk
grated zest of ½ lemon
4 egg yolks
75 g/3 oz/⅓ cup caster sugar
50 g/2 oz/½ cup flour, sifted
15 ml/1 tbsp rum or brandy
25 g/1 oz/2 tbsp butter
200 g/7 oz savoyard biscuits or 300 g/11 oz
   sponge cake, cut into 1 cm/½ in slices
75 ml/3 fl oz/5 tbsp Alchermes liqueur
   or cherry brandy
75 ml/3 fl oz/5 tbsp Strega liqueur
45 ml/3 tbsp apricot jam

TO DECORATE
fresh whipped cream
chopped toasted nuts

1 Heat the milk and lemon zest in a saucepan. Remove from the heat when small bubbles form on the surface.

2 Whisk the egg yolks. Gradually add the sugar and beat until pale yellow. Beat in the flour. Stir in the milk, through a strainer, and pour into a heavy saucepan.

3 Bring to the boil, whisking constantly. Simmer, stirring constantly, for 5 minutes. Off the heat, add the rum or brandy and the butter. Allow to cool, stirring to avoid a skin.

4 Brush the biscuits or cake with the Alchermes liqueur or cherry brandy on one side, and the Strega liqueur on the other.

5 Spread a thin layer of the custard over the base of a serving dish. Line with a layer of biscuits or cake. Cover with some of the custard. Add another layer of biscuits.

6 Heat the jam in a small saucepan with 30 ml/2 tbsp water. When it is hot, pour or brush it evenly over the biscuits or cake slices. Continue with layers of custard and liqueur-brushed biscuits or cake slices. End with custard. Cover with clear film or foil, and refrigerate for at least 2–3 hours. Serve, decorated with cream and nuts.

Walnut & Ricotta Cake

Torta di Noci e Ricotta

Soft, tangy ricotta cheese is widely used in Italian desserts. Here, it is included along with walnuts and orange to flavour a whisked egg sponge. Don't worry if it sinks slightly after baking – this gives it an authentic Italian appearance.

Makes 10 slices

INGREDIENTS
115 g/4 oz/1 cup walnut pieces
150 g/5 oz/⅔ cup unsalted butter, softened slightly
150 g/5 oz/¾ cup caster sugar
5 eggs, separated
finely grated rind of 1 orange
150 g/5 oz/⅔ cup Ricotta cheese
40 g/1½ oz/6 tbsp plain flour

TO FINISH
60 ml/4 tbsp apricot jam
30 ml/2 tbsp brandy
50 g/2 oz bitter or plain chocolate, coarsely grated

1 Preheat the oven to 190°C/375°F/ Gas 5. Grease and line the base of a deep 23 cm/9 in round, loose-based cake tin. Roughly chop and lightly toast the walnuts.

2 Cream together the butter and 115 g/4 oz/½ cup of the sugar until the mixture is light and fluffy. Add the egg yolks, grated orange rind, Ricotta cheese, flour and walnuts and mix together.

3 Whisk the egg whites in a large bowl until stiff. Gradually whisk in the remaining sugar. Using a metal spoon, fold a quarter of the whites into the Ricotta mixture. Carefully fold in the rest of the egg whites.

4 Turn the mixture into the tin and level the surface. Bake for about 30 minutes until risen and firm. Leave to cool in the tin.

5 Transfer the cake to a serving plate. Heat the apricot jam in a small saucepan with 15 ml/1 tbsp water. Press through a strainer and stir in the brandy. Use to coat the top and sides of the cake. Scatter the cake generously with grated chocolate.

Coffee Granita
Granita di Caffè

An ice crossed with a frozen drink, a granita is solid, not slushy. Make it in a food processor.

Serves 4–5

INGREDIENTS
475 ml/16 fl oz/2 cups water
115 g/4 oz/½ cup granulated sugar
250 ml/8 fl oz/1 cup very strong
   espresso coffee, cooled
whipped cream,
   to decorate (optional)

1 Heat the water and sugar together over low heat until the sugar dissolves. Bring to the boil. Remove from the heat and allow to cool.

2 Combine the coffee with the sugar syrup. Place in a shallow container or freezer tray, and freeze until solid. Plunge the bottom of the container in very hot water for a few seconds. Turn the mixture out, and chop into chunks.

3 Place the mixture in a food processor with metal blades, and process until it forms small crystals. Spoon into tall serving glasses and top with whipped cream, if desired. If you do not want to serve immediately, pour the mixture back into a container and freeze until serving time. Allow to thaw for a few minutes before serving, or process again.

Lemon Granita
Granita di Limone

Nothing is more refreshing on a hot summer's day than a fresh lemon granita.

Serves 4–5

INGREDIENTS
475 ml/16 fl oz/2 cups water
115 g/4 oz/½ cup
   granulated sugar
grated zest of 1 lemon
juice of 2 large lemons, plus peel to decorate

1 Heat the water and sugar together gently until the sugar dissolves completely. Increase the heat and bring to the boil. Remove from the heat and allow to cool.

2 Combine the lemon zest and juice with the sugar syrup. Place in a shallow container or freezer tray, and freeze until solid. Plunge the bottom of the frozen container or tray in very hot water for a few seconds to loosen. Turn the frozen mixture out, and chop it into large chunks.

3 Place the mixture in a food processor fitted with metal blades, and process until it forms small crystals. Spoon into serving glasses and decorate with twists of lemon peel.

Right: Coffee Granita,
Lemon Granita.

Olive Bread *Pane con Olive*

Olive breads are popular all over the Mediterranean. For this Italian recipe use rich oily olives or those marinated in herbs rather than canned ones.

Makes two 675 g/1½ lb loaves

INGREDIENTS
2 red onions, thinly sliced
30 ml/2 tbsp olive oil
225 g/8 oz/2 cups pitted
    black or green olives
800 g/1¾ lb/7 cups strong plain flour
7.5 ml/1½ tsp salt
20 ml/4 tsp easy-blend dried yeast
45 ml/3 tbsp roughly chopped parsley
    or mint

1 Fry the onions in the oil until soft. Roughly chop the olives.

2 Put the flour, salt, yeast and chopped parsley or mint in a large bowl with the black olives and fried onions and pour in 475 ml/16 fl oz/ 2 cups hand-hot water.

3 Mix to a dough using a round-bladed knife, adding a little more water if the mixture feels dry.

4 Turn out on to a lightly floured surface and knead for about 10 minutes. Put in a clean bowl, cover with clear film and leave in a warm place until doubled in bulk.

5 Preheat the oven to 220°C/425°F/ Gas 7. Lightly grease two baking sheets. Turn the dough on to a floured surface and cut in half. Shape into two rounds and place on the baking sheets. Cover loosely with lightly oiled clear film and leave until doubled in size.

6 Slash the tops of the loaves with a knife then bake for about 40 minutes, or until the loaves sound hollow when tapped on the bottom. Transfer to a wire rack to cool.

VARIATION: Shape the dough into 16 rolls. Slash the tops with a knife and cook for 25 minutes.

Index

First published in 1999 by Lorenz Books © Anness Publishing Limited 1999

Lorenz Books is an imprint of Anness Publishing Limited,
Hermes House, 88-89 Blackfriars Road, London SE1 8HA

This edition published in Canada by Raincoast Books, 8680 Cambie Street,
Vancouver, British Columbia, V6P 6M9

ISBN 0-7548-0036-9

A CIP catalogue record for this book is available from
the British Library.

Publisher: Joanna Lorenz
Editor: Valerie Ferguson
Series Designer: Bobbie Colgate Stone
Editorial Reader: Kate Henderson
Designer: Andrew Heath
Production Controller: Joanna King

Recipes contributed by: Angela Boggiano, Roz Denny,
Nicola Diggins, Joanna Farrow, Shirley Gill,
Jeni Wright.

Photography: William Adams-Lingwood, Karl Adamson,
Edward Allwright, Steve Baxter, James Duncan,
Michelle Garrett, John Heseltine, Amanda Heywood,
Janine Hosegood, Michael Michaels

Printed and bound in Singapore

1 3 5 7 9 10 8 6 4 2

Notes

For all recipes, quantities are given in both metric and imperial measures and, where appropriate, measures are also given in standard cups and spoons. Follow one set, but not a mixture, because they are not interchangeable.

Standard spoon and cup measures are level.

1 tsp = 5 ml
1 tbsp = 15 ml
1 cup = 250 ml/8 fl oz

Australian standard tablespoons are 20 ml. Australian readers should use 3 tsp in place of 1 tbsp for measuring small quantities of gelatine, cornflour, salt, etc.

Medium eggs are used
unless otherwise stated.